THE DOWN ENTREPRENEUR

A Blueprint To Business Rejuvenation

Duane Jones
with Nikki Gillis

LAEL PUBLISHING

THE DOWN ENTREPRENEUR
A Blueprint to Business Rejuvenation
by A. Duane Jones
with Nikki Gillis

Published by Lael Publishing, LLC
Winston-Salem, North Carolina
www.LaelAgency.com

ISBN 978-1-7325344-4-5

First Edition

Printed in the United States of America.

DEDICATION

The greatest gift is the gift of service to the ones we share a heartbeat with: our children. Being a single father has taught me so much and I'm proud to say I still haven't graduated yet. Although I love all of my children, this book is dedicated to my firstborn: my daughter, daddy's baby girl, KD. Who would have known a preemie baby, born 2 ½ months early, would endure and grow into such a fine young lady? Through all the hard times including multiple moves, going without, and all the unknowns, you stayed sweet, strong, and smart. You truly felt the side effects of daddy working hard to create a life for us. We've both pushed through sicknesses, emotional distress, countless let downs, isolation, and the list goes on and on. But one thing is for sure: we always had each other. I'm all the more blessed to be your father because of the hardships we faced together. I want to thank you for continuing to be a major reason to keep pushing forward in this journey called life.

Love Daddy,

TABLE OF CONTENTS

PREFACE

Everybody's got the juice, or at least that's what they say. If you want the blueprint to success, just go and ask so and so. If you want the keys to the city, just do this or that. Who really can say what the path looks like for "The Down Entrepreneur"? The idea of success is defined by many, BUT the steps to unstoppable success are outlined by few. The real outcome is determined by your effort.

I may be a lot of things but taking personal jabs at someone isn't my style. So, scratch that thought from your mind. This book isn't about detracting from others. Instead, it is a collection of the most powerful lessons I have learned from my life experiences. With my years in the entertainment industry, I've seen a lot and dealt with much. To some, I'm a celebrity photographer. To others, I'm the homie Duane. But to my three seeds, who are affected by all my decisions whether I choose right or wrong, I'm a role model. Therefore, it's important to me to get this out, not only for them, but for anyone else who may be struggling.

It's been on my heart to share some wisdom for my everyday people who have dreams, ambitions, and hopes of becoming the next _________. I don't want us to see each other differently because our passions aren't the same. I love and have a passion for food, photography, and mentoring kids. You, on the other hand, may love music, acting, or teaching. Bottom line: We all have a passion. Whatever your passion, if you're hungry enough, you will be unstoppable if you follow some key steps.

I've set this book up as a journal for you with an

execution point (meaning: put into action) for each action. Anyone who wants to be successful and get the results they long for will need to fully execute a plan, stick with it, and not be so quick to give up easily. It doesn't matter what action you start with, a space to jot down your notes has been included for you with each action point. This will be short and sweet. Besides, a brother gotta get back to shooting the next great ______. Oh, I'm serious about this filling in the blank thing! You guys are going to work today, just like me! Let's get started.

ACTIVATION POINT 01

GET UP

I know you're reading this like: You can't be serious Duane. Get Up?!!! I'm serious as can be! The number one thing we go back and forth about in our head is when to actually get up, show up, get counted present, and do the job!! We get hyped by so much daily, whether it's our favorite song, quote, work-out routine. But once that fizzles down we're still laying in the bed! The hardest task you'll confront as you start your journey to entrepreneurship is to GET UP! The mere thought of simply getting out of bed each and every day to give yourself a new start can seem so overwhelming! For most of us, it feels like we just laid down. Look at it this way: Once you do it, you've completed the hardest part of the day.

So many entrepreneurs are so saddened and suffocated with depression and anxiety that they keep to themselves because most people judge these emotions as a weakness. There's nothing weak about admitting how hard this road is. YOU decided to put everything and everyone on the back burner and do something for you!!! That alone is a major accomplishment!! Unfortunately, you can't expect everyone to relate and understand that. But you still have to know it for yourself.

Each day you sit on the edge of that bed, make your mind up to put your feet down to the floor and get up. It will feel like a mission accomplished! It makes me think of the saying, The early bird gets the worm! The ones who get up and show up for success eventually win! Add a little twist to your routine: Get up an hour earlier than normal to give yourself room for more opportunities for success to reach you! There are big wins out there in this world with your name on them. The more you put yourself in a position to receive them, the more you'll be ready when they show up in your life!

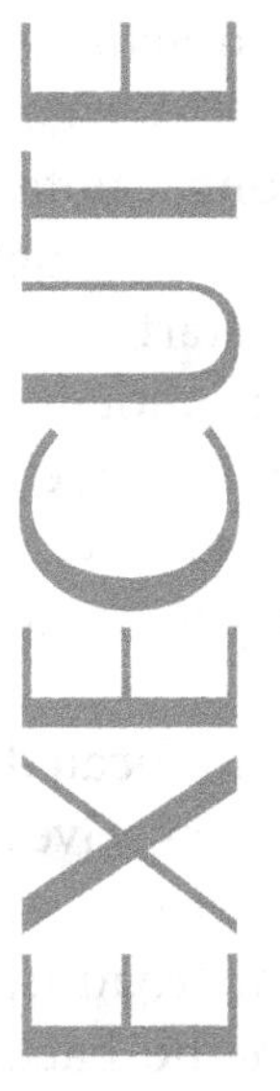

Using your blank journal sheet on the next page, think about your current routine for getting up. Write it down, study it, and look at it honestly. I know all about setting the clock fifteen to twenty minutes early so you can sleep in for a few more minutes on snooze, but what else could you be doing with those few minutes? Could you possibly get up thirty minutes to an hour earlier to motivate yourself for the day? This time is for you, to sit, to meditate, to think and prepare yourself for the day. If you're really amped, take those minutes and get a little work-out in there or read something very uplifting for your mind to be in a position to handle whatever happens that day. Remember, it's a mentality you're working towards here. It's going to take work, but it can be done! Start off by pushing yourself to GET UP!!!

ACTIVATION POINT 02

ADMIT YOUR CONCERN

You can have mountains to climb but not know what equipment to use to even start the process. In most situations, there will always be some areas that cause you to pause and consider the difficulties you may face. For example, you believe you have a million dollar business but you do not know all the logistics involved in handling the processing of your items. You truly have a concern. The most important part is that you know there is a concern and you are admitting that to yourself. The interesting thing about admitting your concern is that it can be in the beginning of your journey as an entrepreneur, in the middle of your journey, or right on the eve of your big win. The truth of the matter is, having concerns is a normal part of the process of doing anything worth doing, so don't worry too much.

It makes me think of my grandma. She always used to say, "If it doesn't feel like you're going through something, then the devil is winning!"

I'll admit, I never truly understood that UNTIL I started

on the path of working for myself. You are a business owner now, so admit that to yourself, and admit that at times you'll undoubtedly have concerns about your business and the nature of its immediate success. This concern can take over your mind and control every thought that enters your brain. Trust me, this too is normal. It's so important to remember in this phase that it is more mental than anything else because you're embarking on something new that you can't see the outcome of yet.

Although this problem or concern that has surfaced is bothering you, keep in mind that someone, somewhere else, is in a worse predicament than you. It doesn't diminish your concern, but it does put it into perspective and will assure you that you're not alone. This is a good time to be brutally honest with yourself and admit your weaknesses just the same as you know your strengths, because it's going to take a balance of both to get you through this moment. Being realistic with yourself will help you to know if this is truly a concern or just a moment when you're scared and one of your fears is pushing itself forward.

Are you creating a problem where there's really not one present? Hence in actuality, having concerns is a good thing. It helps you keep things balanced and prevents you from pumping up your own head too much.

Using your blank journal sheet on the next page, write down your current or last concern that was bothering you about your business. Now, looking at this concern in written form, ask yourself a few questions: What are the facts about this concern? What are the possibilities with this concern? Now weigh the difference.

It's always good to address the hard facts first, BUT keep in mind the possibilities. A lot of times we get carried away with the possibilities, or the what if's, that they overpower the facts of the concern we need to address. Be sure that you're writing this down so you can retrieve it at a later time.

If you compare this current concern to the previous one, are you noticing a pattern, or are they similar? This will help you distinguish if you really have a true concern or a moment of panic due to the uncertainty of the business and this journey. Keeping a log of these concerns can help you recall them so you will know how to solve them the next time or help someone else who may find themselves stuck there as well.

ACTIVATION POINT 03

PURSUE YOUR PASSION

How many of us gave any thought to what most of the older people in our life tried to tell us when we were younger or growing up? Here are some of the things they said which may sound familiar: "Go for yours. You can achieve anything. Pursue your passion. When you love what you do, you'll never work a day in your life."

Now remember, in this book, we're going to keep it real and not sugarcoat things. For the majority of us, we may recall these words of wisdom and realize we didn't listen or believe them at the time. It seems kind of sad, but sometimes we put ourselves through some of the toughest moments just to realize something we heard before and we didn't listen to or believe was actually true. By this time, we're ready for a change! We're ready to go all the way!! We'll take that risk! Once you condition your mind to KNOW that these words or sayings are achievable, the world of success opens for you!

Pursuing your passion is a very important aspect on your map to entrepreneurial success. When I think back on my career moves, working in finances and teaching were cool, as they did relate to my love for people. However, it was once I began my mission of becoming a photographer that I blossomed, not only in business, but as a man, period!! Many creative entrepreneurs like myself get an itch around the third to fifth year mark of any job. After that period elapses, there's a deep yearning to take steps towards what is truly meant for us. I found myself bored out my mind and very unhappy at these jobs as time passed. It resulted in me being written up several times and called to the principal's office as a teacher. Although I was working full time as a photographer, the teaching job felt like a parachute. The comfort of having a day job left a superficial sense of security. I still wasn't fully emerging into what I knew I could be, and I needed to be happy. Reality is, when I left that job and began doing what I knew in my heart I LOVED, the flood gates slowly but surely opened up. To me, the rest is history!

Using the blank journal sheet on the next page, write down what you LOVE to do. Your passion can be one thing or a combination of things, but it ties back to you. On the back side, write down what you're currently doing and how it may relate to what you love. Each day, do one thing that helps you take a step closer to doing what you love. When you love what you do, everything counts. It's important to remember that feeling of happiness inside that you experience when you're doing what you love may sometimes come without being paid for it. Keep in mind, you're taking steps daily to get closer to what you really want to do and never allow anything to stop you. Make now the time that you decide to reroute things so that you are taking steps to pursue your passion!

ACTIVATION POINT 04

BE THANKFUL

If you're like me, there have been times when you lost sight of what's really important throughout this journey to entrepreneurship. One of the most important things to keep in mind is that there's always something positive to be found in every situation we face. Hence, in all things, BE THANKFUL!! When the going gets rough, we find ourselves being pessimistic about the outlook. The costless thing you can do that will save you heartache and pain is to be thankful for it all! Change your mindset and be thankful for the rainy days and storms just as much as you smile upon the sunny days and your focus will not waver! One of my favorite pastors had an amazing saying that I've always kept close to my heart.

He'd say: "What you focus on, you move towards!"

This is the perfect opportunity to apply the principle of cause and effect in life. Think of it this way: By constantly focusing on negativity, you'll produce more negativity or find yourself surrounded by it or those types of people. However, if you're constantly focusing on positive things, you're bound to be more productive, and even during trying times, you're bound to yield positive results.

Another way to sum this up is called the Law of Attraction. Now you won't find many people just walking around smiling, waiting for the next negative thing to happen, but you will find people who are better prepared when it comes. They know how to work through it. Remember, it's only temporary. Be thankful for the trying times on this road to achieving success.

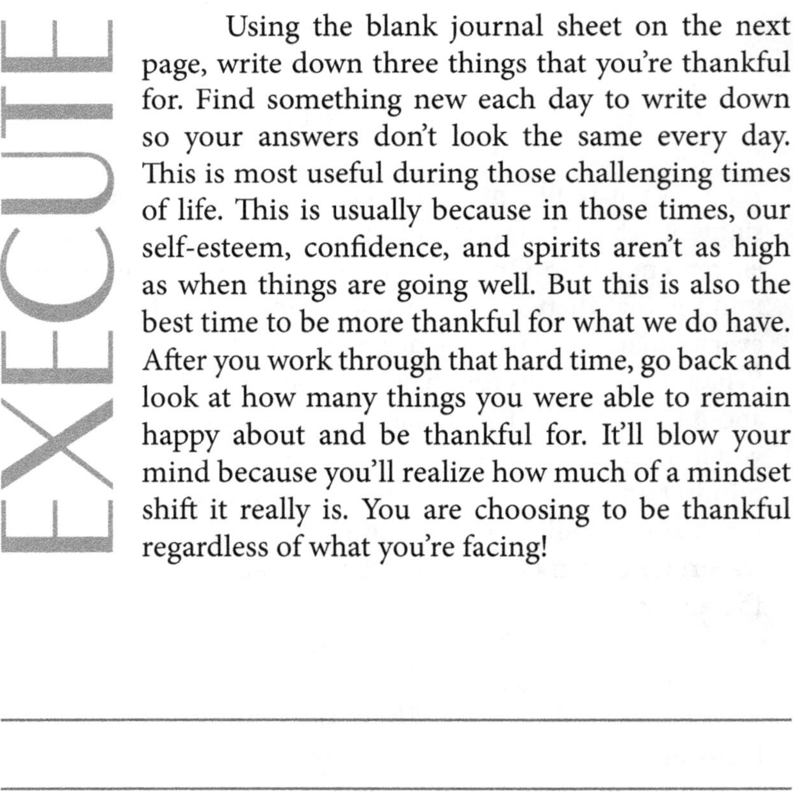

Using the blank journal sheet on the next page, write down three things that you're thankful for. Find something new each day to write down so your answers don't look the same every day. This is most useful during those challenging times of life. This is usually because in those times, our self-esteem, confidence, and spirits aren't as high as when things are going well. But this is also the best time to be more thankful for what we do have. After you work through that hard time, go back and look at how many things you were able to remain happy about and be thankful for. It'll blow your mind because you'll realize how much of a mindset shift it really is. You are choosing to be thankful regardless of what you're facing!

ACTIVATION POINT 05

CURSE A TREE

So far, all this sounds good and you're geared up and ready to give it your best right?! Well, that's until you hit a dead end, so to speak. Ultimately there will be times when you hit a wall. You started something new, you left a job, failed at a major task, weren't getting the progress you expected, etc. You try your best to push past it and remain focused, but you're literally on the edge. Do not, I repeat, do not internalize those frustrations!

It has often been said, the things we speak of have a way of manifesting, so even if you're irritated, be mindful of what you say. I know you're reading this and thinking I'm crazy because I haven't addressed how you deal with your dead end. First, you must confront it and get it out of your system. Then, you must release somehow and somewhere! In order to retain your sanity and avoid taking your grief out on clients, friends, or even family: GO FIND A TREE AND CURSE IT OUT!!!! That's exactly right, I said it, find the meanest, ugliest looking tree and let go! Just run if it starts talking back to you!! The longer you hold on to that dead weight, the slower you'll start to move. As Down Entrepreneurs, we must always be moving forward. Stress and grief are like athletic ankle weights. Unstrap them and see how much better you maneuver on your journey!

Now this is one time I want you to leave the blank journal sheet on the next page blank UNTIL you've completed this exercise. Go to the bathroom and write down each ugly thought holding you prisoner on tissue paper. If you want, be cost efficient and jot a couple of them down on the same block of tissue. Once you have all the thoughts you feel are slowing you down, stand in front of the toilet, say those words on the sheets of tissue out aloud, and flush them all down the toilet. The key is to allow yourself to feel the release and most importantly to watch it go away. That way, your mind mentally registers that you can't retrieve it back! That's the goal that you want! Just imagine if you had written it down in this book, then you're not mentally or visually letting it go. Your brain will hold those thoughts captive and the thoughts will just resurface another time! So, go ahead, we'll get more tissue later! Flush those thoughts away and guess what? YOU'RE STILL CURSING A TREE!!!!

ACTIVATION POINT 06

GIVE YOURSELF DAILY DECLARATIONS

Now, I know someone is reading this and saying to themselves, What in the world are daily declarations? Look at it this way, daily declarations are a two part process. The first part of this process is to ask yourself a series of affirmation questions. Notice the following questions: Who are you? What are you doing each and every day to accept who you are? How successful are you? Whose business is this? Who do you believe in?

The answers to these questions are the second part of the process and are the proclamations you must declare daily. You must learn to speak these things into existence consistently. Declare your positive standing and the actions you'll take to make them real. This will not only serve as a method to adapt, but you'll also create a mental road map to achieve success.

EXECUTE

Once you have an idea of the direction you'll go, then write out those items you need to affirm daily. Place them right here in this section on your blank journal sheet on the next page. This too is a section you will revisit from time to time throughout your entrepreneurship journey. Once you have the questions, practice reading AND answering them aloud. MAKE THIS A HABIT!!!!

A Blueprint to Business Rejuvenation- Activation Point 6

ACTIVATION POINT 07

CHANGE YOUR PERSPECTIVE

If you don't remember anything, remember this: You're in control of your mindset. The one thing you can always do for free, in any situation, is to be open to changing your perspective. This reminds me of the "glass is half full" theory. What you don't have has no bearing on what you do have.

You are what you eat, correct? Equally so, you are what you think. You have the unique ability to think in a way that gives you strength or makes your feel weak. Your mind is such a strong tool. With this tool, you must use it positively and effectively.

If and when you find your mind adrift, you must consider that at some point you have been in a trying situation before. Instead of gloom and doom thoughts, focus your energy and mind power on methods that can help you better gain control. For lack of better words, CHANGE YOUR PERSPECTIVE! If you can't afford a certain item you feel will help your business grow, try to rent it or borrow it from a colleague. Instead of feeling down about a potential ally telling you no, find others that will fill the void and align with them. Your mindset should never be a CAN'T, a WON'T, or a NEVER! You can, you will, and your efforts are coming to fruition sooner than you think. Keep the faith. Lead your mind to a place of positivity.

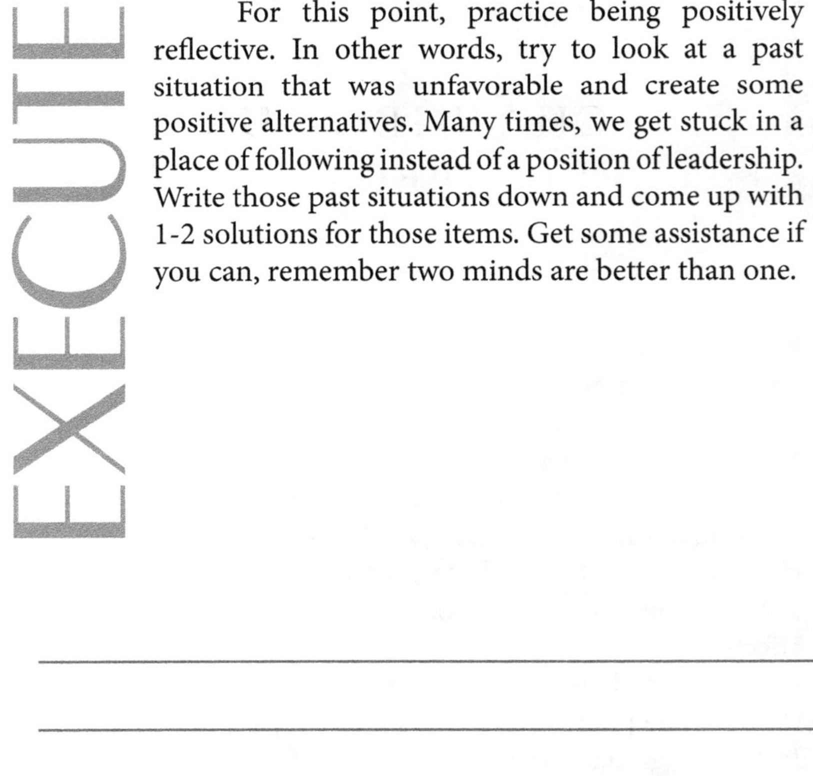

For this point, practice being positively reflective. In other words, try to look at a past situation that was unfavorable and create some positive alternatives. Many times, we get stuck in a place of following instead of a position of leadership. Write those past situations down and come up with 1-2 solutions for those items. Get some assistance if you can, remember two minds are better than one.

ACTIVATION POINT 08

BELIEVE

A vital key to your success is your belief in your vision. No one, I repeat, no one will love your vision more than you! We've all been hopeful for something before. Just reading that already spells out to me something every Down Entrepreneur will eventually face: doubt.

If you are in a place in your business when business is not going as planned, you must PUSH FORWARD. In order to push forward, you must first believe. We often contribute hope to this magical fairytale type of luck. It's that familiar old got one foot in the door if it works and the other foot out the door in case it doesn't work kind of logic. We must change that hope to belief. When you believe in something, the conviction is strong and can't be easily shaken. Believing is unwavering, undeniable, and KNOWING that what you desire will come to you! Your belief is tied to your skills and your skills are what you are putting into action. You start doing something not only because you love it, BUT because you believe you will succeed in it. Believing is only half the battle, the rest requires action on your part to work towards bringing your dreams to life.

EXECUTE

Using the blank journal sheet on the next page, write down what you believe in. This means no amount of money could change your faith in it. By writing it down, this will help you build your faith even stronger in these things that you hold dear and valuable to your heart. Make it a practice to visually read over this list at least once daily.

ACTIVATION POINT 09

CLAIM IT

This may be a little harsh for some people, but we are all grown folks here, so let's go. A hood rule: Scared money don't make money! This simple concept applies to business ownership globally. In essence, you must honestly ask yourself: How can I receive what I need if I never ask for it?

Think back to when we were kids. How many times would you do something without asking someone because you wanted to prove a point? You wanted to prove to the adults that you were capable and could do things on your own. Now as adults, let's be honest, we keep that mentality going but the root thought can also stunt our growth. In business, we seldom ask for help and many times we are too prideful or timid to ask for things we want.

So, what's the point of all of this? KNOW WHAT YOU WANT AND CLAIM IT!! Know your passion well enough to be well versed on who in the industry can help you. Everyone is not meant to be your mentor or the person who can truly help you. Find the person or people that are able to assist you. Now go for it!

EXECUTE

This is definitely an eye opener for you. Write down the things that you're coming across in your business that you find are hard to ask for help with. Please be very honest with yourself because if you don't, they will resurface, and show up in your business routine and how much you're thriving. Worse, they are likely to show up at a time that is inconvenient for you.

ACTIVATION POINT 10

PLAN LIKE YOU ARE "MEAL" PREPPING YOUR MIND

Believe it or not, accountability is a huge part of success as an entrepreneur. I know it sounds cliché, but there must be some structure in order to achieve your goals. Simply put, those that don't plan, plan to fail.

Think of it in terms of food and how well we prepare for that when we're trying to do better or save money. Break down your daily, weekly, and monthly goals as if you were planning your meals for a period of time. All the foods we love to pig out on, usually aren't the best for us. The same applies with your goals. Be sure to keep a healthy balance when planning your goals. There will be some you can easily attain, while others may take some time to reach, but work towards giving them your best effort.

Be sure to strategize so you can stay progressive with your goals. An example for me when it comes to the tasks involved for a photographer is editing. Editing to me is like telling kids they have to eat veggies before having a cookie or ice cream for dessert. They know they want the latter part but in order to get it, they have to face that part of eating the veggies. The parents win because they're continuing to show their children the importance of being balanced in eating. The kids win because they had to overcome something they'll later appreciate in life, but they also get to enjoy their dessert. I don't jump and do my happy dance to edit, but I know it's a valuable part of the process of photography. Therefore, I incorporate time for editing on the schedule at my agency. And, I apply the same principle to the other less favorable parts of my work to make sure I stay on top of every aspect of my business.

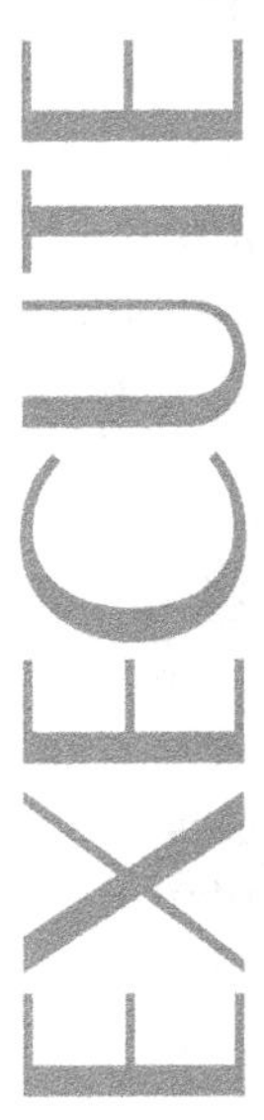

Use the blank journal sheet on the next page to write down each day of the week. Then add a weekly view, as well as a monthly view. Take your goals by short and long term and fill them in according to your schedule now. This picture won't come together right away. You might stare at the blank paper for a minute until the thoughts start rolling in. This is exactly how you want it to be. You'll notice, depending on how important those goals are to you, you may have to change or alter a few things around to achieve them. This is the mentality you want to adapt. You want to see the finish line with them. Look at what is taking up time in your schedule now, put them in place, and knock them out!!!!

This is an example of what your goals would look like, based on the information you input for your business. Everyone is different, so set them according to what you can realistically accomplish.

Days of the Week:

Sunday	Monday	Tuesday	Wednesday	Thursday	Friday	Saturday

Days of the Week and Monthly Dates:

Sun.	Mon.	Tues.	Wed.	Thur.	Fri.	Sat.
5/5/19	5/6/19	5/7/19	5/8/19	5/9/19	5/10/19	5/11/19

Short/Long Term Goals:

Short Term Goal	Long Term Goal
Call 5 potential people a day	Convert at least 25 people a month from call list

Status of Achievement (did you complete, need improvement, additional notes)

Achieved	Need Improvement	Additional Notes
Y/N	Y/N	

Weekly/Monthly View of Goals (you decide which works best for you)

Day	Date	Short	Long	Achieved	Improve	Notes
Sun	5/5/19	Call 5 potential people a day	Convert 25 people a month from call list	Y/N	Y/N	
Mon	5/6/19					
Tues	5/7/19					
Wed	5/8/19					
Thurs	5/9/19					
Fri	5/10/19					
Sat	5/11/19					

ACTIVATION POINT 11

STEP OUTSIDE OF THE BOX

Organization simplified!! In order to grow through a struggling, new, or underperforming business, you need to reach out to people. You must use the law of large numbers to assist with obtaining results. If you want to gain new business, the most obvious task would be to reach out to people. In the age of technology, we have a zillion methods to get in touch with potential clients and market our business.

It's just as important to know your target audience. You have a service or product that they don't know they need yet. How can you present it to them if you don't know who your main audience is? Knowing who to target with your advertising will be critical to keeping those costs down by making each contact more likely to convert into a sale. Use text, emails, social media, or face to face interactions to solicit new business.

EXECUTE

Use the blank journal sheet to write down at least 5 to 10 contacts today that you will reach out to. Take a look at that list and think about who you personally know vs the ones you may not be acquainted with. The reason for this is to decide upon how to approach them. For the ones you know, think about how they communicate. Are they better with texts, emails, or calls? If possible, it's important to learn people's communication style. It will help you tremendously in your business. It's even good to follow up with the ones who were uninterested from time to time if they're your target audience, because people's needs change daily. A "No," can turn into a "Yes" the next week!

ACTIVATION POINT 12

KNOW YOUR WEAKNESSES

Questions: What in the world is wrong with you? Do you even know?

These are a few of the questions that run through your mind when your weaknesses show up in business!! We are great chefs, doctors, photographers, etc., BUT we may not know jack about some of the things that will come up in business!!

Most times, people want to showcase their strengths and hide their weaknesses. Seriously, if you don't know what you are weak at, how can you grow?

In marketing, there is something called a SWOT Analysis. SWOT stands for: Strengths, Weaknesses, Opportunities, and Threats. In EVERY aspect of your business, you should and must do this simple assessment. As you see, weaknesses are listed!

It's almost like back in the day when we were kids and that special someone caught our eye in class. We'd send a note that said check 'Yes' if you do like me and will go out with me, or 'No' if you don't. That simple note taught us to prepare ourselves for both answers back then without minimizing one! It's the same process with SWOT. Write down all your strengths, opportunities, weaknesses, and threats. From those, you should be able to see a clear map of where you stand and what needs to be tweaked or improved. You must be honest and look under every rock to ensure you're making a fully informed decision.

Use the blank journal sheet to write down what you know your weaknesses are. Then directly across from it, write down a strength you have that you can use to combat that weakness. Please understand this is a learning process. You can't write down everything one time and think you have it right! It takes time, and it'll teach you a lot about yourself. It's also helpful to consult a trusted friend or colleague whom you know will be honest with you and in return, you will listen to their feedback. Be open to writing their responses of what they feel are your strengths and weaknesses. Are there similarities? Did you both say a few of the same things? In either case, work at it, because what you don't confront about yourself will surface in your business and usually not in a good way.

ACTIVATION POINT 13

MAKING MISTAKES ARE INEVITABLE

Now don't get in your feelings about this one, but as the saying goes: Those who don't learn from history are doomed to repeat it!

In this age of technology, everything seemingly changes overnight! We not only cannot do the same things repeatedly, but we also must stay ahead of the trends. Thus, learn from your mistakes!

The most successful businesses take a few risks, but these risks must absolutely be calculated. If a segment does not work in business, we must take note and adjust accordingly. The key is to take ownership of your mistake, but at the same time, be mindful of the other factors that play a vital role. Who are we surrounded by? Are all business relationships best for your business? Who are we listening to in business? These are all questions we must ask ourselves from time to time as we embark upon this journey. Also, we must learn from our errors. Don't beat yourself up for making a mistake or not seeing something. We aren't perfect, so accept that.

EXECUTE

Use the blank journal sheet to write down the last three things that went wrong or not so well in your most recent business venture. That is, if you're already in business or you're on the road of preparation to do so. What situation happened that you could learn from? Can you admit your fault or the role you played in it? Now that you've admitted your part, what other factors can you take into consideration? Always be mindful to write down the facts of the situation. Not the opinion or one-sidedness, but the facts. The facts will keep you from taking it too personally when it's not only about you. This is your business, so there's more at stake here.

ACTIVATION POINT 14

SECURE A MENTOR

Now here's a necessity. Find and secure a mentor within your industry or the industry you're attempting to enter. Now there's a little trick to it. In business, you're always told to be in quest for knowledge. In most cases, experience does matter, so this can be a difficult task. The key is to find someone within your industry that has been there before, so to speak.

Let me offer an example from my life. I have two mentors that serve in different capacities. One is a cheerleader and my main source of inspiration. To a degree, I can do no wrong in that person's eyes. This is good for two reasons: Their good vibes will keep up my motivation and watching this mentor in action gives a blueprint to what will and won't work for me. The other mentor is the straight shooter! This one tells me like it is! This is the most important mentor to have on speed dial.

A mentor who will tell you what you're doing wrong and show you how to adjust accordingly while still being true to who you are (and not just who they want you to be) is priceless!! Notice that the best mentors know you, how you roll, and are able to adapt their perspective and advice to what is going to best work for your particular style, strengths, and weaknesses. There are millions of mentors and although you must find who's right for you, be sure you're finding someone who's adaptable to teaching you. That's an art not mastered by many!!

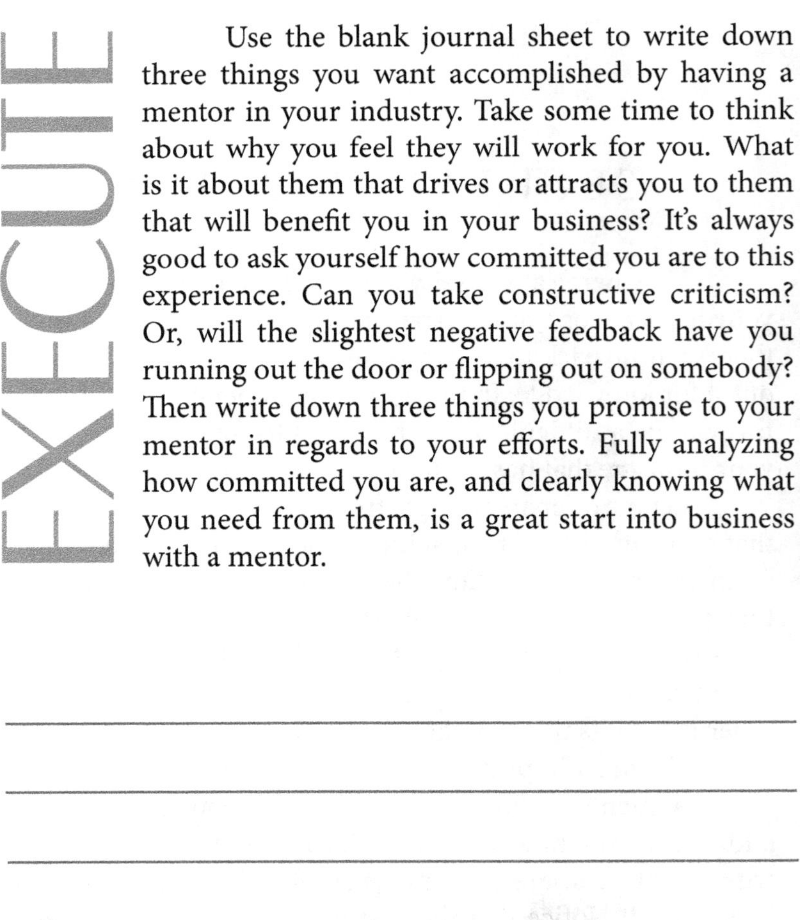

Use the blank journal sheet to write down three things you want accomplished by having a mentor in your industry. Take some time to think about why you feel they will work for you. What is it about them that drives or attracts you to them that will benefit you in your business? It's always good to ask yourself how committed you are to this experience. Can you take constructive criticism? Or, will the slightest negative feedback have you running out the door or flipping out on somebody? Then write down three things you promise to your mentor in regards to your efforts. Fully analyzing how committed you are, and clearly knowing what you need from them, is a great start into business with a mentor.

ACTIVATION POINT 15

STAY POSITIVE

One of the easiest pitfalls of entrepreneurial life is that of being pessimistic. Spending time in this mental state of being is self -sabotaging! I've had many days in which I told myself at the beginning of the day that no one wanted to buy anything from me, or that people just didn't support my business. Those thoughts internalized into reality, and yes, precisely because I spoke it into existence.

However, there are things you can do to work through this tough mental state of being. First thing in the mornings, say your "I Am" affirmations. "I am great! I am productive! I am going to have a great day!" Put your mind into a place of positivity and you'll see it manifest in due time. Even if your day seems to be a bit challenging, you'll see your mind is more apt to work on solutions instead of wallowing in self -pity.

EXECUTE

Use the blank journal sheet to write down three of your favorite "I AM" affirmations about yourself THAT YOU BELIEVE WITH NO CHANCE OF DOUBT!!! Yeah, I know, that made you pause for a minute. We're so accustomed to hearing this talk and seeing it on social media, BUT that last part gets you every time. What are the ones that YOU believe to be true? Take it a step further and place them on your mirror, in your car, on your desk at work. Place them in areas that you frequent daily so you're setting your eyes upon them and then pausing to internalize what it feels to see those words, know you believe them, and allow them to inspire you to give it the best effort you have! This molds your mindset for positivity!

____

____

____

____

____

____

____

____

ACTIVATION POINT 16

UNDERSTAND THAT YOUR BEST FRIEND IS 'NO'

Now I know you're reading this and wondering: Where is he going with this?! But I promise you read that correctly. Your best friend is 'No.'

Now I won't tell you who to pick as your best friends, and no I don't want you to tell me who they are, BUT I am telling you one of them needs to be a two -letter word we hate to hear sometimes, NO!! Stick with me here! Business can be ruthless at times. As you grow, know that even if you are a Down Entrepreneur, business can and will be demanding. You must set in your mind how to appreciate this word in two parts. The first is being told 'No' by potential customers, and the other being told 'No' by business owners who don't see or appreciate your vision! Now, does that mean they're stupid or crazy for not wanting to lock arms with you, or appreciate what you can bring to the table for them? No, it doesn't!! Hearing 'No' is a daily part of business life!

Please don't let this be the step you decide to get into your feelings about. I promise, you'll be hurt or disappointed each time! 'No' is that nagging fly that you just can't seem to swat! BUT the more you get used to hearing it, the more appreciative you'll be in hearing a 'Yes' when that time comes! I know you're wondering if I have any clue of what I just wrote, but I must reassure you, I do!! There's a mindset that isn't designed for anyone when it comes to 'No.' It takes a lot of nerve, patience, and persistence to keep going when you're hearing 'No' ninety-nine percent of the time.

But think about what is it teaching you. Is it showing you that you must be serious about what you are in business for. How much do you believe in what you're doing? It definitely sounds contradictory, but 'No' is an absolute necessity in business. Bottom line: 'No,' is always preparing you for 'Yes!!!' "Yes, I want your business! Yes, I want to work with you! Yes, I believe in your vision!!" YES, YES, YES, begins with NO, NO, NO!!

Now here's the flip side to 'No.' It is necessary to say 'No' sometimes in business. When you first start out, you're excited and hungry for the business, so you 'Yes' to any invite, any networking gig, or project, mostly unpaid, barter, or low pay. I see the light bulbs going off in your heads now. As you grow in business, you realize how important it is for you to say 'No,' sometimes because it doesn't serve you any purpose or isn't needed for you to grow! Now there's a method to this one too, BUT we'll tackle that later!

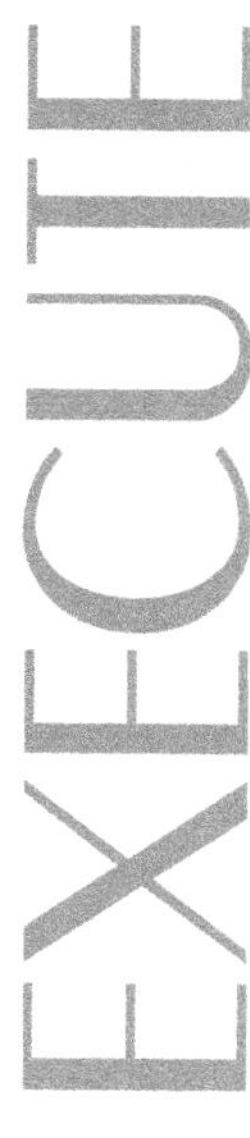

Try this exercise. Take a deck of cards and shuffle them. Quickly turn over one by one as fast as you can. For every Ace, say "Yes!" and for every other card, say out loud "No." Imagine you are hearing these answers from potential clients. Sure, there are lots of "Nos", but the "Yeses" always eventually come, sometimes sooner, sometimes, later. Practice not taking the "Nos" personally. After all, it's just a numbers game. Take time and celebrate the "Yeses" because sure as the sun comes up, a "Yes" is right around the corner.

ACTIVATION POINT 17

BE MINDFUL OF DREAM KILLERS

How many times have you heard the saying: Birds of a feather flock together?

If you're still in denial, or just don't quite believe it is true, try separating yourself and focusing on your passion and see who starts to kill your dreams with their non-support! It happens to all of us at one time or another in business. We thought so and so was our friend, that they believed completely in us, until we opened our eyes and saw the truth!

Remember this, there will NEVER be anyone that will love your vision as much as you do!

With that being said, you must keep reality in mind at all times. The reality is that most people truly do not wish to see you become more successful than them. It's a sad fact, but it's very true, and normally one of the first three people who will show their true colors is someone very close to you and in your circle. Now, not to sound contradicting, but the majority don't wish to see you fail, even though some do. Most just don't care to see you doing better than them! Hence, they revert to being dream killers! Your ideas to them will not be feasible or practical enough. You will hear some of the most disappointing statements from these people.

Go ahead and prepare yourself; it's bound to happen! You have to remember it is about the mindset and the will power to go ahead and do step 1; GET UP!!!! (See Activation Point 1) That alone will separate the majority because we all complain, whine, and groan about something in our routine in life. HOWEVER, not everyone wants to truly put any actions to doing something about it. Before they watch you smile, and feel inner peace and happiness, they'll ridicule, dictate, and destroy your dreams IF you allow them to! Please don't think they come in one category. No. They can be found in family, friends, significant others, neighbors, church members, and co-workers. In a nutshell, surround yourself with dream builders and dream chasers, NOT the Dream Killers!

You have to be quick about identifying Dream Killers early on. They are always wearing their true colors, you just don't normally see them because you rarely voice what you desire to do from the heart and place yourself on the path to do it. Once you identify them, don't try to change them or argue with them. HEAR their words as you can't control when they will say, but be quick to dismiss their negativity BEFORE internalizing it. Let them know in a calm manner you appreciate them expressing their thoughts, but you are doing what is best for you.

Don't be tempted to go into giving a long explanation; stick to your beliefs and dismiss yourself from their presence. This is a good time to pull out your daily affirmations and say them out loud to yourself. Once you're away from them, take out your affirmations and repeat them to yourself. Doing this will help you not internalize and not question yourself about what they said. If you allow yourself to internalize their negative words, you will stay there mentally and it's like being paralyzed. Remember this vision is crystal clear to you only, so do what you have to do to protect it!

ACTIVATION POINT 18

GUARD YOUR TEMPLE (EAT WELL)

You must take care of your temple. For those who may not be familiar with the word temple, in this sense, I'm speaking of your body. Every day something is being added to the list of what not to eat, and sometimes it's food we once thought to be healthy. Therefore, we must be mindful of what we consume in our bodies! The stats on fatty meats, high fructose corn syrup, etc. are scary enough! I know it brings back the memories of hearing our parents fuss about what we need to eat, but it's absolutely true. Healthy eating benefits us in the long run.

On this road navigating as a Down Entrepreneur, you'll find some of the ugliest truths about yourself because sometimes you probably operate in anxious mode. Some days you'll look up and realize you didn't have a substantial amount of food or fluids to nourish your body. I know somebody will read this and think Not me!, but I promise you, I said the same thing at one time.

Be conscious of researching the right nutrition for you

and your body. Don't focus too much on what you like and don't like, simply put, eat what's healthy as much as you can on a consistent basis.

Use the blank journal sheet to write down what you've eaten in the last three days. If you can go further back, write that down too. Keep a written list in order to resort back to it, to trace your patterns and pick one food to replace with something healthier. Do this for a month so you're getting a complete look at what you're consuming. It has been proven it takes twenty one days to kick a bad habit, so put yourself in a position to work at this, one food at a time. If the meal isn't keeping you energized naturally or helping you stay focused but instead it's causing you to be sluggish or negative, REPLACE IT!

ACTIVATION POINT 19

EXERCISE

Now that you've started somewhere, and most likely it's with what you eat, you have to combat that with another positive routine: EXERCISE! This will keep the body in shape and young, but exercise will also relieve some stress. Stress has been known to be the number one killer for years now and we all can do our part to work at controlling that.

Let me be the first to tell you, there's nothing like having a gloomy day and the thought of knowing soon you are going to the gym to work all that out is so refreshing! Whether your routine is weights, the punching bag, or machines, it's all exercise and it shows you care about you! Self-care is beyond important in this journey. Our bones and muscles aren't designed to last forever, so we have to do our part in keeping them as balanced as we can. Exercising regularly will give you the strength and energy to keep pushing and operate your business in the best capacity, even on the most challenging days.

EXECUTE

The success of this point depends on your answers to a few questions. If you already exercise, could you add more to your routine? If you don't exercise at all, could you start out with thirty minutes a day or at least three times a week? This is one of those things where there is always room to improve, so write down your plan so you can see it and work hard to stick to it. It's a great opportunity to get an exercise buddy, someone who will help keep you inspired and do it with you.

ACTIVATION POINT 20

GO TO BED

Now I'm about to get on somebody's nerves, but simply put, take your tail to bed at night!!! As an entrepreneur, there is always the urge to burn the midnight oil and keep working! The facts are, there are only twenty-four hours in a day, and the majority of us have that planned out. So, calculate some much needed time to sleep and do so peacefully.

A sufficient amount of sleep gives our body the chance to rejuvenate. Think of it this way: Sleep is also your time to DREAM!!! I've had the most productive ventures and outstanding ideas pop up into my mind while I was asleep. They turned out to be great for my business! It helps me stay confident in my grind, but most importantly, a balanced routine of sleep keeps me focused! Life is already busy with planning this and that. Taking a little catnap somewhere during the day can be a good thing!

EXECUTE

Use the blank journal sheet to write down how many hours of sleep you are currently getting and record this daily for a week. Go back and analyze these numbers and realistically look at the activities that are keeping you from getting more sleep. Ask yourself, what can you do to increase that time so that you're getting a minimum of eight hours a night? Are you using simple remedies such as a good hot shower before bed? Perhaps a good lavender oil or lotion works just as well since lavender is known for giving the body the calm effect, preparing the body to sleep. There are many cost-efficient things you can do to give your body the rest that it needs to prepare well mentally for the next day. It all starts with looking at where most of your time is being spent now.

ACTIVATION POINT 21

STACK YOUR COINS (SAVE)

If it's one thing I know, it's that pennies make dollars and dollars make sense! The easier translation would be: SAVE, SAVE, SAVE!!! Most businesses are cutthroat, and sometimes, it's feast or famine. The reality is, you may be good at what you do but poor with business practices, such as finances and saving sufficient funds to cover every aspect of getting started. Therefore, saving is an integral practice that is necessary for your business to ultimately grow.

There's one mentality you should lock in place early on, and that is to save as much as you can, whether things are going good or bad. I know that's easier said than done, but think of how much harder it is to do once things are bad and you feel you need the money. It's always a good practice to save at least ten percent of your earnings for rainy days or those "just in case" moments. These funds shouldn't be touched unless it's extremely important. Never base running your business off wants, base it off of what is needed for the business. Placing these funds in an account that isn't easily accessible will help you in the long run.

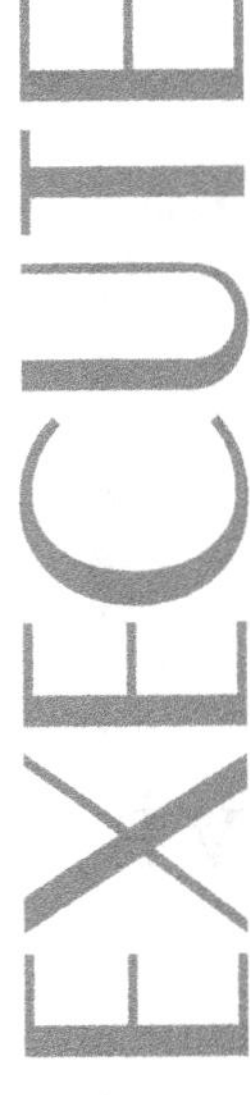

This will be very hard for some, but it's the gut right truth. If you can't be extremely honest in asking yourself how good are you with saving, then you may benefit better by having your mentor or accountability partner answer it for you. If your eyes are always bigger than your budget, and you can't afford to pay for it instantly or have necessary funds set aside to carry out your plans, you need to make some MAJOR adjustments!

The beauty is if you find this to be your case, no need to beat yourself up, put forth every effort to correct that toxic behavior; it is not good for business. If you have a trusted mentor or friend, allow them to keep track of the funds you set aside. Always be willing to expand your knowledge and sign up for a few business classes at your local community college or institution of your choice. It's going to be rough, but if you need to eat oatmeal for breakfast every morning and have peanut butter and jelly sandwiches for lunch daily, do what you need to do to save for your business!!! The idea is to grow the business, so there's a lot of discipline that comes with that if you are headed for success.

____

____

____

ACTIVATION POINT 22

KEEP UP WITH THE JONESES

For the sake of this book, Keeping up with the Joneses is simply staying two steps ahead of the technology curve. Technology is a vital part of business whether we like it or not! Think of it this way, you wouldn't dare drive your car around without airbags, anti-lock brakes, and any other standard requirements for safety, would you? The same applies in business.

The technology world is accessible to us all, however, what we do to keep up with it for our industry is up to us. Nowadays, we know Facebook and Instagram are popping. Are you trying to operate your business off the same Myspace account you had 15 years ago? I hope you answered that with a resounding "No!" You would apply this same rule with your business as an entrepreneur. Stay in the know of the latest and most useful technological advances being brought out in your field.

In my field as a professional photographer, the industry changes daily. Cameras and new software come out more often than the latest iPhone. It's imperative to take the time to research and learn the new technology in your field. You will always thank yourself later for the effort you placed in finding out what's new, what will improve your business, and what makes your clients feel like doing business with you!

Think of how all entrepreneurs have standard business cards. From a marketing standpoint, what would make your card stand out better amongst the other cards on the shelf? It's all in the basic things that are easy to overlook. The thickness and type of paper it's printed on right on down to asking yourself if your message is clear as to what it is that you do. Is the customer easily able to contact you from the info on the card? Think of it from your client's standpoint, THEN explore how creative you can be to set yourself apart. That is the wow factor that keeps you separate.

Use the blank journal sheet to write down the last technology tool you investigated or used for your business. Ask yourself is there something else out better than that now? What are the top performers in your industry using? Are you open to try some other tools to get an idea of whether they can help you or not? This is the time to write down everything that you can think of to go back and explore to see where you can improve. It's a never-ending story in learning about your industry so keep your thinking caps on.

ACTIVATION POINT 23

KNOW YOUR MARKET

There are questions that never get old, and you'll find yourself asking them often no matter how many years you've been in business. Do you know what your clients need? Are you listening when they tell you what they need? Do you care to see where your business lines up with their future needs?

One way to think of it is looking at when changes occur globally, affecting us all in some way, such as tax reforms, legislation, technological advances, or healthcare concerns. A solution to combat the changes that affect your industry would be to subscribe to the leading standard publication in your sector so you're always in the know. When you do, don't let these publications sit on the coffee table and collect dust; make it a habit to pick them up and read them. If they're the leading publication in your industry, they'll be filled with information needed for you to stay afloat and on top of your competition.

Also, it's a good idea to join the professional organizations that lead the way in your industry. People change daily, which means policies, tools, and rules change too. When I was living in North Carolina, I couldn't stand Instagram, as I was a

Facebook head. When I relocated to Georgia, I was informed that Instagram was a major business factor there. For the first two years, I focused extensively on building my Instagram account with a little under 2,000 followers to now over 10,000. Now, the market that I'm in can see more of what I do. That's knowing your industry.

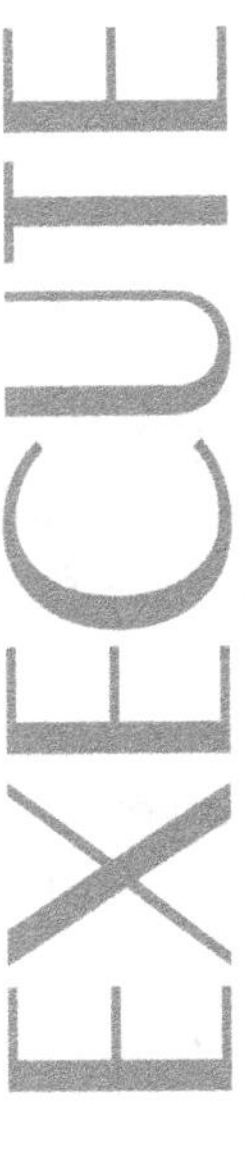

The quickest and most effective way to do this is to pick one platform to study and build trust with your clients. Engage with them, liking their posts, commenting when you feel it's necessary, and reposting. Read the top blogs in your industry to see what your clients are needing. Trust me they'll tell you. People love the opportunity of being heard but the key is to realistically listen if that's your target audience. Being genuine goes a long way, so be real in your interactions with your audience. Don't be afraid to step outside the box, no need to fit in! You're wanting to build trust with them so look at your business to see what you can offer them free. People love giveaways! People love free information or the feeling of getting something for free! It truly works so give it a shot!

ACTIVATION POINT 24

DON'T BE THE SMARTEST

Golden rule: You should never be the smartest person in your life. Within your industry, there's always someone with more knowledge than you. Seek those people out and learn from them. As the saying goes, You're as strong as your weakest link. Be sure it's the two-fold factor, too. They possess the knowledge, but they also should possess the hunger to want to know and learn more; they don't easily become complacent in their business. My personal motto: I am loyal as a puppy to those in business, BUT the moment we stop moving forward is the day I move on. I'm smart enough to know that if we aren't progressing, then we're regressing! Take the time to research people just like you research your craft. Now that's smart!

EXECUTE

Take the time to research people in business matters. A lot of people talk a good game, but sooner than later, their true intentions always surface. Give it time; they'll show themselves. The people who are a fit for you don't always have a title behind their name as being the best in this or that. Some people you just meet along the way. Sometimes, it's the most unlikely person that you can learn the most from. Loyalty is a key quality, but so is your word. Remember, it's your business, so that clear vision is seen mostly by you. If you're open, the right people will surface in your life that need to be alongside you in this business. Appreciate those people. Most times, we can't easily replace them.

ACTIVATION POINT 25

FIND SOME QT (ME TIME)

We all can agree: Down Entrepreneurs run hard!!! We go for what's ours and will not stop until we get it! Through all this hustle and bustle in life, we must find 'Me Time.' If you're sleeping, eating, and exercising right, you still must find time to do the things you enjoy, other than work. You'll feel at your best and help your mind to refresh when you're doing something that pertains to replenishing your cup for you!

What are your hobbies or things you like to do in your spare time? What activities come to mind that automatically put a smile on your face? These are things you'd call 'Me Time.' They help you remember you and celebrate yourself in all that you are accomplishing. They might include playing with the kids, going bowling, watching a movie, or reading a book. All work and no play makes the day go grey! You can't afford to lose yourself chasing your dreams and not taking sufficient time to enjoy your life along the way. In a nutshell, don't ignore yourself or family/friends trying to be Superboss!!! You will miss and need them at some point in life.

EXECUTE

Since everyone's make up is different and what works for one doesn't work for all, do this at your discretion. No matter what, set aside thirty minutes to an hour daily to just do nothing or reflect on you and what you're feeling. Add a hobby you enjoy in this mix such as the ones noted above BUT try to focus on the ones that require alone time. Break it up, thirty minutes alone, reflecting, then take the other thirty minutes and read a book, listen to music, play with the kids, or enjoy some quality time with your significant other. As much as you can help it, give yourself solo time or solitude. There's a mentality you want to adapt to in appreciating you, where you currently are, and where you're going.

ACTIVATION POINT 26

LOCK IN ACCOUNTABILITY PARTNERS

There have been plenty of times as a Down Entrepreneur that I've felt alone. Sometimes, in business, you feel alone, no matter what your industry is. This is one of the main reasons why I tell people all the time this work isn't cut out for everyone. Staying within that feeling of being alone too much is where irresponsibility can surface or the slip ups come in! Thus, you need an accountability partner!!

The need to be held accountable for our decisions and goals in life is mandatory. In most cases, for those who have a spouse or significant other, it's that person. I've also seen cases where people keep it separate and it's not that person. The reality is, the accountability person is your straight shooter! They're going to give it to you raw and unfiltered so that you get back in line. We all lose focus sometimes in business and this person helps us keep our head in the game BECAUSE they truly believe in us, even when we don't believe in ourselves!

This person truly supports your dreams and will be there

beside you to cheer you on. You need someone in your corner to keep you flowing fluidly with your goals. We're imperfect, so those people help us remember the tasks we forget. They remind us of the end goal. They keep us motivated and give us great insight. Everyone needs at least one AP (Accountability Partner) in their corner!

EXECUTE

Use the blank journal sheet to write down the top six people who you personally know who inspire you. We all have a celebrity or public figure that we look up to, but that doesn't mean we can pick up the phone and call this person when we need to, so these people need to be among those you know.

After you think of these top six people, start narrowing them down by asking yourself a series of questions. Does this person genuinely have my best interest at heart? How do they deal with me when I make a mistake or if I'm wrong? Life calls for our feelings getting hurt, but do they tell me what I need to know to benefit me or help me in the future? How do I feel when I talk to them or when I'm around them? How much of my vision or dream do they support, meaning the good, the bad, and the ugly? As you ask yourself these questions, your answers will change and you may be left with three or less people. These people should be one of your AP people or on your AP team!

ACTIVATION POINT 27

STICK TO YOUR GUNS (STAY FOCUSED)

The shortest distance between two points is a straight line. However, that doesn't mean that it's going to come easy and in a flash! As an entrepreneur, I've fallen victim of this shortcoming many times. Most entrepreneurs are creative beings, this usually means that at times we're known for deviating from the plan. Some of you are nodding your head in agreement while others are in denial. The truth is we all fall short of sticking to our guns at times and the quicker we can recognize it and correct it, the better off we'll be. At times, we love coming up with great ideas, BUT we will often abandon a plan or idea to do something else. The coming up with great ideas and plans is a good thing, but it's not so good if we haven't finished most of the things we've started! We have to learn to tough out the uncomfortable moments so as to follow through a plan until our goal is reached.

A famous Buddha saying goes: Change is hard at first, messy in the middle, and beautiful in the end.

I urge you to make your plan and stick to it because simplicity is the key! After you do your planning and projecting, set your goals and follow through with them. There's nothing wrong with adding complimentary pieces at times but getting overwhelmed and ahead of ourselves by going in different directions, stopping and starting, may cripple our progress.

This is the meat of this book, the main reason why this blank journal part was inserted for you. Write, write, write!!! If we write out our plans, we're more likely to stick to them. When you visually look at what you wrote out, and add pictures or drawings to help bring it to life, you're usually motivated to stick to it. The bottom line is we see the work that needs to be done, we see the destination or end results, and most importantly we see ourselves doing it! Understand how important it is to stick to the plan, and how necessary a visual plan is!

ACTIVATION POINT 28

RESEARCH AND PLAN

Please understand that knowing is only half the battle! When it became crystal clear that I had reached my business ceiling in North Carolina, I began researching other cities and states. Although the decision to relocate to Atlanta wasn't easy, it ultimately was the best decision for my kids, my business, and life! I wouldn't have come to appreciate any of that process had I not done my research and took the time to investigate the area and market.

It was a toss between Charlotte and Atlanta, but Atlanta offered me the biggest opportunity for potential business growth. Do understand that plan involved multiple visits to the area before I made the jump. In business, I couldn't move then get the ball going in rebuilding my business. No. I had to hit the ground running before relocating! When the time came for me to move, I had a small but consistent clientele already established. Plus, I kept my business in NC. So, plan, prepare, and execute!!

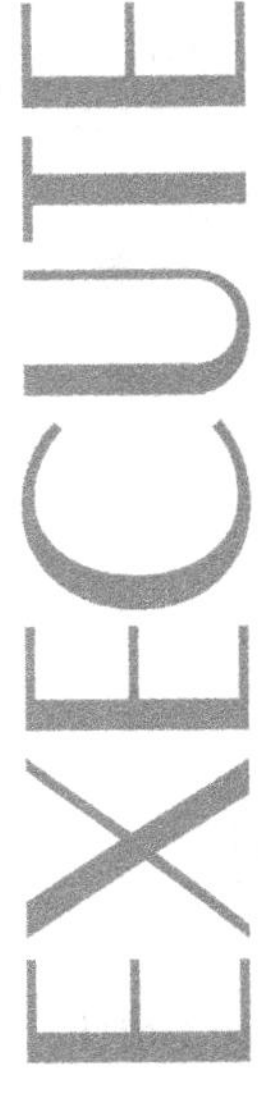

As stated, knowing is half the battle because the rest consists of you being in action! When you take the time to prepare, you increase your chances of multiple successes AND recognize the success doesn't stop there! Keep going! Keep planning for that next win and execute how you'll get there!

We all love the feeling when people see and compliment us on our success and sometimes the hype around it gets us distracted. Caught up in the hype, we may have decided to sit and chill and enjoy the noise we're making. Instead, we should always be humble in appreciating it and plan for what's next because it's all short lived. No one ever plans a business to make it big one time then go sit down. With that success comes more work and strategic planning to achieve our next level of accomplishments.

I can't encourage you enough to utilize the tool of writing. Write down here on the blank journal sheet to your right, three short and long term goals you'd like to see in your business. Whether it is to hit five thousand in followers, book six clients repeatedly each month, or make ten thousand in profit monthly, write down these goals, then put the plans together to execute them!

ACTIVATION POINT 29

MAKE UNREASONABLE GOALS

I was always told that your vision should be bigger than you. If that's the case, then your goals should be lofty. Most creatives build to be helpful or because they see a need or a void they can fill. I'm almost certain the creator of Amazon never expected the online sales of books to turn into the most profitable revenue in the world, BUT I bet he set out a goal to make the most of that platform that he could! Therefore, having unreasonable goals allows us to never become stagnant.

There is always some task to conquer when your goals and dreams are ginormous. My initial goal of having three studios nationwide started with one being in my living room. I now have two, one in Fayetteville, NC and one in Atlanta, GA. It's two down one more to go! I wanted the ability to frequently travel while fulfilling my dream of providing epic photography to fellow creatives worldwide. I'm living that and I haven't stopped, so who knows what's next after I add that third studio location! Crunch time! Let's go!

EXECUTE

Use this time to really think about what you can accomplish right now in terms of short term goals and then set even bigger ones based off those to continue achieving! Setting the bigger goals drives the momentum in achieving them! Think of the wildest thing you dream of happening for your business. Ask yourself why this dream is so wild? Then, think about who put the limitations on that dream and said it's not possible? Was it you? Map out a strategy to make that unreasonable goal come true. You can do this and it's out there waiting on you!

ACTIVATION POINT 30

WRITE DOWN YOUR VISION AND GOALS

I know by now you're tired of this five-letter word popping up repeatedly: WRITE. I hope it is sinking into you how serious this step is. Even with dreams, research, and aspirations, you must WRITE down your vision and goals!

You've probably heard of a vision board before. There's not any magic trick to it, but it's exactly what it's called. The purpose of the vision board is to help you execute these goals. It takes time and real effort to put together your vision board, so usually that means you're serious about doing the work.

I remember being a kid and all of us piling up in the car to travel to New York to visit family for the summer. I couldn't imagine traveling to the state of Northeast Ohio through the depth of upstate New York without utilizing a map. Remember, there was no GPS back then either. A drive of that magnitude without a map could take forever! The same concept goes for your business. Map out your goals and overall vision so that once you start the planning and implementation phases, you have a clear direction to see it all the way through!

EXECUTE

Some may call this childish, but in business, you'll be surprised at some of the things we do that remind us or take us back to the elementary days. Find yourself a basic map, something easy and appealing to you. Take the time necessary to look at it, study the different angles, and all the tools on the map for you. What stands out to you, and what seems interesting to you? Use your own sticky notes or something personal to you to cover up certain areas with your goals. Rename the map, place that unreasonable goal or two at the end. Take notice of the pathways and work involved to reach that goal. No, it won't be perfect, but the idea is to get your creative juices flowing in your brain to start seeing how realistic this can be for you. Make it yours and dedicate yourself to doing the work to see it through and reach your dreams!

A Blueprint to Business Rejuvenation- Activation Point 30

ACTIVATION POINT 31

KNOW YOUR PURPOSE IS BIGGER THAN YOU

Whatever you do in life, you must know that your purpose is bigger than you! When those times come where you want to hit the snooze button one hundred times, or you just don't have the confidence to pick up the phone and call a potential client, remind yourself someone needs what you have. See your product as a product in high demand and it is up to you to get the word out there about it.

Most times, we don't have to look far to see that need. For me, my kids need me. I can look at their cute little faces and know that I have a bigger purpose than just myself. I've built contacts and relationships with countless wardrobe stylists, make-up artists, chefs, and so forth. My success is a must because others are attached to my success! We all can win! I can't be weary when I know my creativity will ultimately help someone else!

EXECUTE

Use the blank journal sheet to write down three things bigger than you as to why you must succeed! It can be your children, you parents, your spouse, or significant other. Maybe it's that one teacher who believed in you, or someone you lost in death and can't tell them how much their support meant to you. Think of the expressions on their faces when they see you win. How does it make you feel? Are you motivated to keep going and tackle the next big thing on your list? Take out your daily affirmations and repeat them to yourself to deepen that purpose. Now go out there and give it all you got!

BONUS POINT 

PICK AN OUTSOURCE METHOD

One of the most influential pieces of information you could use in business is obtaining someone's email address. Let's add to that and say, gather as many cell phone numbers as you can too. These two valuable pieces of information are the tools you need to create a meaningful relationship with a client or potential client. It's all about serving their needs and gaining their trust! Although people may occasionally ignore phone calls, most of us all read our text messages and emails. I take this approach because you never know when a 'No' will turn into a 'Yes'! Make it a habit to remember people's names, they can tell when you sound like a salesman or if you're taking a personal interest in them. At all costs, don't spam them either! That's the quickest way to lose a client!

BONUS POINT

STEP INTO THE ROOM (PASSION)

How many of us remember being told as children we could be anything we wanted to be, whether that was a lawyer, police officer, doctor, president, etc.? My parents showed me through their hard work that success was possible. As I got older, I quickly realized, if you love what you do, you'll never work a day in your life!

Now let's be honest, there are days that you won't feel this way all the time; it's part of life. There are days that I despise some things about being a professional photographer. People ask me all the time how I personally feel about college and if it's necessary. I didn't ultimately need to go to college to be a professional photographer, as I spent one hundred dollars for a class at a community college in South Carolina and learned most of the fundamental skills within that one class. We see so much in the world today. Some spend years and years in education and by the time they get out, they can't find a job in that profession or they are told they are overqualified. That alone can be depressing because you think of all the time you've spent and wonder if it was wasted.

My point is this: With the world rapidly changing, I highly recommend EVERYONE own their own business to some capacity! Find your passion and get paid doing what you love. Think about it, when it's your passion, you'll naturally gravitate towards the education you need, whether it's some classes at a community college or whatever route you chose. Too many companies are holding our futures in their hands and dropping them when they feel like it. Job security is too shaky now. One thing I do know is, I will never fire myself! If I want a promotion, I can work for it and immediately get it! My performance directly affects my pay. I am in control and I love it! Even during off seasons or hard times, I have opportunities to make money doing what I love and keep rising!

CLOSING

As I close out this book, I ask you to go back and pick out your favorite action points that you can implement now. When I thought of this book, my goal was to provide a short guide in the form of a journal to help the Down Entrepreneur, right now, who is struggling or overwhelmed by information and still unclear where to go next on their journey.

There are so many books out there to help and direct us. Some are by our favorite authors, celebrities, and business moguls. I wanted to show the next business owner just how close they are to their dreams by keeping a few simple steps in mind. Most things we do to shape and mold our success are all built on having or obtaining the right mindset. I wanted you to personally fill in your profession on that empty spot in the preface because it's your dream to fulfill and I believe you can do it! You are the Down Entrepreneur and your journey is one for the record books because it's yours!

The best part about this is, as previously stated, you don't have to follow this book in order, feel free to skip around, and the principles still apply as they are. It's short and small enough to keep in your backpack. Pull it out and jot down the notes you need, to take you to where you desire to be, in your personal journey of entrepreneurship. And if ever needed, just look me up on social media when you're ready and I'll add that dynamic headshot of you to your portfolio.

My motto is: "We Shoot to Kill!"

Take this blueprint into entrepreneurship seriously, give yourself the time you need to rejuvenate, and your success will be unstoppable. Just as you wildly dreamed it to be! It's waiting for you. Go get it!

ABOUT THE AUTHOR

Antoinne Duane Jones with his motto, We SHOOT to Kill! echoing throughout social media, there's no question that it can be traced back to Atlanta's Hottest Celebrity Photographer. Duane knows firsthand how cutthroat success can be in the entertainment industry. He began as a finance manager, found himself teaching marketing in public high school for five and a half years, then later transitioned fully into photography. He is passionate about sharing his tools for success with those who are committed to becoming the entrepreneur they have dreamt of being. His motivating style emphasizes the fact that it doesn't matter the field or industry, the mindset of success is still the same. The Down Entrepreneur takes things a step further by offering the reader a practical thirty-one-day countdown to use to achieve this mindset. It is a direct and no-nonsense approach designed for the average person to achieve success by changing their outlook, one simple exercise at a time. Duane can always be found with his weapon in his hand, his camera, shooting the next business mogul who's down with the entrepreneur life and knows when to rejuvenate!

www.ingramcontent.com/pod-product-compliance
Lightning Source LLC
Chambersburg PA
CBHW071701210326
41597CB00017B/2283

* 9 7 8 1 7 3 2 5 3 4 4 4 5 *

THE DOWN ENTREPRENEUR

A Blueprint To Business Rejuvenation

"The idea of success is defined by many **BUT** the steps to **unstoppable success** are outlined by few."

Ask any upcoming or prosperous entrepreneur and all will agree, **it's a hard knock life out there!** The moment it enters your mind to put your best foot forward and pursue this path everything changes. You tell yourself this can't be real because it's so much you don't know; the uncertainty feels bigger than the vision. You look to your right and left and the people you thought would be on the sideline cheering for you are gone. You've been told no so many times you're starting to think you've been cursed. You've seen your fair share of insufficient funds and overdrawn bank statements. Somehow through it all, your drive to keep going is an untouchable force. You'll never forget what it felt like to hear that first yes! When you think of red, it's a thing of the past now because you're seeing green and it's never felt so good! You looked to both sides and can't believe the faces you recognize standing there with you doing a praise dance! The truth of the matter is, this is all a part of the plan!

The purpose of this book is to help you outline a few necessary steps to unstoppable success and rejuvenate yourself while doing so. It doesn't matter where you are in this journey of entrepreneursh[ip]; pick any chapter in this book and apply the point EVEN AFTER being successful. This blueprint isn't a one hit wonder and you're set for life, it's a key to help you maintain it and enjoy the benefits it brings. The journal insert allows you to start now putting these practices to use. Wait time is over, let's go!

ISBN 978-1-7325344-4-5
90000
9 781732 534445